# Hot Cars

# MERCEDES

### Lee Stacy

Rourke
Publishing LLC
Vero Beach, Florida 32964

LIBRARY OF CONGRESS CATALOGING-IN-PUBLICATION DATA
Stacy, Lee, 1961-
  Mercedes / Lee Stacy.
    p. cm. -- (Hot cars)
Includes bibliographical references and index.
ISBN 1-59515-212-1 (hardcover)
1. Mercedes automobile--Juvenile litrerature.  I. Title.

TL215.M4S73 2004
629.222'2--dc22

                                        2004014757

For The Brown Reference Group plc

Managing Editor: Tim Cooke
Design Manager: Lynne Ross
Children's Publisher: Anne O'Daly
Production Director: Alastair Gourlay
Editorial Director: Lindsey Lowe

Picture Credits:
IMP AB

Some words are shown in **bold**, like this. You
can find out what they mean by looking at the
bottom right of most right-hand pages. You
can also find most of the words in the Glossary
on page 30.

# Contents

# Introduction

The German carmaker Mercedes-Benz has a proud history. Its parent company is Daimler-Benz, which was formed in 1926 from Daimler and Benz. Those firms had been started by two pioneers of the automobile: Gottlieb Daimler (1834–1900) and Karl Benz (1844–1929). Mercedes cars started to earn a good reputation in the 1950s. By the 1990s Mercedes-Benz was making some of the world's most stylish cars.

*The logo of a three-pointed star in a circle was first used by Gottlieb Daimler in the 19th century.*

*Mercedes' first fuel-efficient small car was the 1997 A-Class. Its size makes it perfect for parking in crowded cities.*

It was helped by its merger with the U.S. company, Chrysler. The cars are also highly innovative. They use cutting-edge technology to achieve performance and safety. Some Mercedes models are already thought of as modern classics. Among these are the luxury S600 and E55 AMG sedans, the C43 AMG station wagon, the CLK coupe, the A-Class town car, and the SLK sports car.

*The SLK is a modern classic. This convertible sports car is one of the most aerodynamic models Mercedes has ever built for the road.*

*The top-of-the-range Mercedes S600 is popular in many places as a limousine for transporting passengers in great comfort. The car has a V12 engine and a top speed of 155 mph (249.4 km/h).*

# Mercedes S600

**D**uring most of the 1990s, the S600 was in a class all its own. Large, luxurious, and powerful, it was popular in many parts of the world as a limousine. It was Mercedes' largest production car, with a **wheelbase** of 123.6 inches (313.9 cm). It also had the biggest of all Mercedes' engines. Even though overall weight of the car was heavy, the V12 engine could accelerate the S600 from 0 to 60 mph (97 km/h) in under seven seconds.

| Vital Statistics for the 1998 S600 | |
| --- | --- |
| Top speed: | 155 mph (249.4 km/h) |
| 0–60 mph: | 6.6 seconds |
| Engine: | V12 |
| Engine size: | 243.3 ci (3,987 cc) |
| Power: | 389 bhp at 5,300 rpm |
| Weight: | 4,960 lb. (2,250 kg) |
| Fuel economy: | 17 mpg |

*The steering wheel of the S600 is trimmed with zebra-wood from central Africa. Zebrawood is often used as part of the decoration in luxury cars.*

## Milestones

**1991**

Mercedes introduces the S-Class at the Geneva Motor Show. The range includes models of different sizes, but all have a V12 engine.

**1992**

The top-of-the-range 600 SEL is given a more efficient 2.8 liter engine. The "SEL" is dropped from the name of the model, which becomes known as the S600.

**1996**

Changes to the S600 include slimmer doors and bumpers painted to match the body.

The huge V12 engine lets the driver know that the S600 is as fast as it is big. Plunge the accelerator and the car steps away, and the five-speed automatic transmission shifts with precision.

The S600 sedan is often used as a limousine because of its luxurious interior. The car's long wheelbase means that there is lots of leg room for passengers traveling in the back.

**Wheelbase**    The distance between the front and back axles.

# Specifications

*Critics have praised the S600 as being the best and most comfortable car in the world. Because of its modified **suspension** system and its **traction**-control system, it gives one of the smoothest and safest rides of any car of the last 15 years.*

### Thicker windows

The side windows on all S-Class models are double glazed. The thicker windows make it easier to control the temperature inside the car. Less outside noise gets in, giving a quieter ride.

### Hi-tech fuel efficiency

The fuel system is monitored by a computer. The computer is housed in a small black box under the hood. It makes sure the engine uses the least amount of fuel possible. This cuts down on fuel wastage.

### Wheel vents

Each of the wheels has five large slots near the rim. The slots help to cool the **disc brakes** inside the wheels.

### Bumper sensors

Sensors in the front and rear bumpers detect how far away objects are. They emit sound waves that bounce back off objects. The strength of the echo tells the sensors how far away the object is. The driver can read the distance on a digital display inside the car.

 On most cars, the doors have to be slammed to shut properly. Those on the S600 have electrical motors that automatically close them tightly.

The interior of the S600 has many electrically operated gadgets, from a sunroof to rear-view mirrors.

## Electronic brake controls

*The S600 was the first Mercedes to use an Electronic Stability Program (ESP). ESP reduces skidding when the car is turning a corner or when the road is wet or icy. It works by controlling the balance between the front and rear brakes and the speed at which the individual wheels turn.*

**Disc brakes** A type of brake with a rotating disc inside the wheel. A clip pinches the disc to stop the wheel.

**Suspension** A system of springs that support a car and make it travel more smoothly.

**Traction** The grip between a tire and the surface of the road.

# Mercedes CLK

In 1998 Mercedes introduced a new **coupe**, the CLK. Designed for sporty drivers, it has some of the best **roadholding** of any Mercedes. It is also very powerful, given that the engine is a fuel-efficient V6. The Mercedes CLK may not be able to reach the top speed of its rivals, the Peugeot 406 Coupe and the Lexus GS 300, but it has better acceleration. It can sprint from 0 to 60 mph (97 km/h) nearly a whole second faster than either.

## Vital Statistics for the 1998 CLK 320

| | |
|---|---|
| Top speed: | *149 mph (239.8 km/h)* |
| 0–60 mph: | *7.2 seconds* |
| Engine: | *V6* |
| Engine size: | *195.2 ci (3,199 cc)* |
| Power: | *215 bhp at 5,700 rpm* |
| Weight: | *3,252 lb. (1,475 kg)* |
| Fuel economy: | *26 mpg* |

*Mercedes used ergonomics to design the cockpit and steering wheel. Ergonomics is the science of making things as comfortable and safe to use as possible.*

## Milestones

### 1993

The midrange C-Class is introduced, with engines of three different sizes: 1.8, 2.2, and 2.8 liters. Only the 2.2 and 2.8 are available in the United States.

### 1997

The C-Class is expanded to include the C240 and C280. Each has improved engines that are more efficient.

### 1998

The CLK coupe is launched. It is based on the C-Class and has a V6 engine.

*The CLK is nimble and responsive, with perfectly weighted steering. Ride and handling have been matched to perfection, and the car comes alive with the V6 engine.*

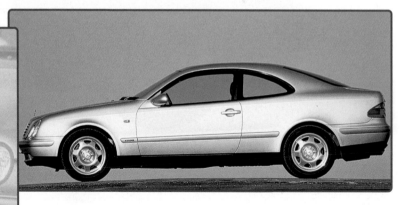

*The top-of-the-range CLK is the 320 coupe. It has a V6 engine capable of producing 215 bhp. This makes the car perform well at both low and high speeds. Although quite large, the 320 handles like a smaller sports car.*

| | |
|---|---|
| **Coupe** | A two-door car that usually seats only two people. |
| **Roadholding** | A car's ability to grip the road without sliding. |

# *Specifications*

The 320 is the top of the CLK range. Although it is only available with a five-speed automatic **transmission**, it rides like a true sports car. The power comes from the V6 engine, which can send the car racing at a top speed of 149 mph (239.8 km/h).

### Oil monitor

The oil level and its condition are monitored by an electronic sensor called the Active Service System. The system also automatically checks the engine's water level.

### Short-stroke V6 engine

The CLK 320 is one of Mercedes' first cars to have the short-stroke V6 engine. This increases the engine's **torque**, which helps to create 215 bhp at 5,700 rpm.

### Controlling wheel spin

The Anti-Skid Control (ASC) on the CLK 320 lowers the engine torque whenever a wheel begins to overspin. This helps the driver to maintain control of the car on wet or icy roads.

 The Electronic Stability Program (ESP) can be added to the CLK. It senses when the car is about to lose control. ESP automatically brakes the wheels and lowers the speed until the car regains control.

CLK's five-speed automatic transmission detects the road's condition and adjusts its shift points accordingly.

### Rear headrests

*The headrests for the rear passengers are large but adjustable. They are designed for comfort and safety. When adjusted properly, the headrest can reduce the risk of whiplash injury.*

### Parking mirrors

*When parking, the side-view mirrors automatically angle downward to give the driver better views of the curb.*

**Torque**      The force produced by an engine to rotate the drive shaft of the car.

**Transmission**      The speed-changing gears that transmit power from the engine to the axles.

# Mercedes SLK

The SLK is a **convertible** sports car first made in 1996. It was designed as a car that would appeal to the upwardly mobile, like its rivals, the BMW Z3 7.9 and the Porsche Boxster. The SLK is one of the most **aerodynamic** road models Mercedes has ever built. To keep the car's body from vibrating at high speeds and on rough roads, the SLK is made from a mix of lightweight magnesium and high-strength steel. It also has an excellent suspension system.

## Vital Statistics for the 1997 SLK 230

| | |
|---|---|
| Top speed: | *143 mph (230.1 km/h)* |
| 0–60 mph: | *7.5 seconds* |
| Engine: | *In-line four* |
| Engine size: | *140 ci (2,295 cc)* |
| Power: | *193 bhp at 5,300 rpm* |
| Weight: | *2,922 lb. (1,325 kg)* |
| Fuel economy: | *17.3 mpg* |

*The SLK's cockpit is compact, but still has room for the extra-large steering wheel that is a Mercedes trademark.*

## Milestones

### 1954

The first SL sports cars, called the 300SL, are launched.

### 1994

The prototype for the SLK sports car is shown at the Turin Auto Show. The new model is influenced by the older SL range.

### 1996

Mercedes begins production of the SLK range. The SLK sports car is an instant success. Demand for the new Mercedes is very high. Critics praise the SLK as a modern classic.

Drive the SLK as fast as you like on rough roads and it shrugs it off. It doesn't flex and it's not deflected from its path. The SLK is small, yet sporty and fun to drive.

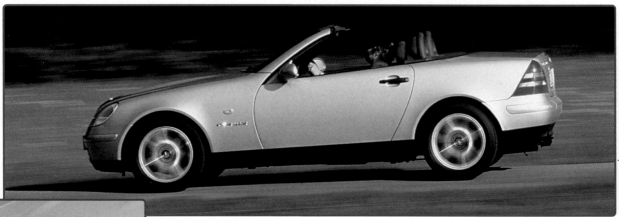

Mercedes made the SLK sleek and aerodynamic. With the top down, the convertible is one of the most impressive-looking sports cars on the open road.

**Aerodynamic**  Designed to pass smoothly through the air.

**Convertible**  A type of car that has a top that can be lowered or removed.

# Specifications

Mercedes named its sporty convertible SLK after German words. "S" stands for sportlich *(sporty)*, "L" is for leicht *(lightweight)*, and "K" is kompakt *(compact)*. The three words perfectly sum up this modern classic.

### Supercharged engine

The all-**alloy** engine has a displacement of 2.3 liters with four cylinders and 16 valves. The fuel-injection **supercharger** gives the engine high power at all speeds.

### Shatter-proof headlights

The headlights are made out of polycarbonate, an incredibly strong type of plastic that is much harder to shatter than most kinds of glass.

 The SLK was designed so that very little wind affects the driver and passenger when the top is down. There is also a wind deflector behind the headrests.

A sensor in the passenger seat detects if a child seat is being used. If so, the air bag does not inflate in an accident.

### Large wheels

To make the convertible appear more sporty, the wheels are very large. They are 16 inches (40.64 cm) wide. Fitting over the wheels are even larger tires.

## Choice of transmissions

*There is the option of either a five-speed manual or fully automatic transmission. Most buyers choose the automatic transmission, because it is easier to use but still knows when the driver is in a sporty mood.*

### Retractable roof

*The hardtop roof on the convertible can be lowered in 25 seconds. Press the button and hydraulic pumps maneuver the metal roof into the trunk.*

**Alloy**    A strong but lightweight metal made by mixing other metals.

**Supercharger**    A device that increases the amount of air in the engine to help it burn fuel efficiently.

**17**

# Mercedes C43 AMG

**M**ercedes first collaborated with engine designers AMG over 30 years ago. In 1998 the two firms produced a station wagon that was more than a high-class people carrier. The C43 AMG is heavy, weighing 3,448 lb. (1,564 kg), so AMG had to come up with a a lot of power. The high-performance V8 engine can send the car racing up to 155 mph (249.4 km/h). That makes it quicker than **sedans** such as the BMW M3 Evolution and the Cadillac Seville STS.

## Vital Statistics for the 1999 C43 AMG

| | |
|---|---|
| Top speed: | *155 mph (249.4 km/h)* |
| 0–60 mph: | *5.9 seconds* |
| Engine: | *V8* |
| Engine size: | *260.3 ci (4,266 cc)* |
| Power: | *302 bhp at 5,850 rpm* |
| Weight: | *3,448 lb. (1,564 kg)* |
| Fuel economy: | *24 mpg* |

*The interior of the C43 is roomy and comfortable but not very stylish. The cockpit, however, gives the driver total control over the car's awesome power.*

## Milestones

### 1967

Hans Werner Aufrecht and Erhard Melcher set up their engine-design company in Grossaspach, Germany. The company's name comes from the initials of the founder's last names, "A" and "M," and of the site of the office, "G."

### 1997

After five years of production, the popular C36 AMG comes to an end. AMG and Mercedes had collaborated on the car.

### 1998

AMG and Mercedes launch the C43 AMG station wagon.

*This is no crude V8 conversion; it's perfectly engineered to the very highest standards. The weight balance is improved, and the stiffer, lowered suspension gives incredible handling.*

*A long wheelbase, a V8 engine, and suspension modified from the Mercedes C-Class range make the C43 station wagon more than just a large people carrier. It is a classic road car.*

**Sedans**     Types of cars with two or four doors and seats for four or more people.

19

# Specifications

For the C43, AMG used the Mercedes C-Class body and **chassis**, but they made major changes to some of the hidden parts of the car. They fine-tuned the suspension, for example, to give a far smoother ride.

**Traveling comfort**

State-of-the-art technology makes the front seats as comfortable as possible. They automatically mold to the shape of the driver or passenger.

**Large, lightweight engine**

The V8 engine is exceptionally large, but because it is made of alloy the engine does not make the car's front too heavy.

**Front suspension**

The front suspension includes coil springs, telescopic **shock absorbers**, and anti-roll bars.

**Large rear wheels**

The rear wheels are 8.5 inches (21.59 cm) wide, while those in the front measure only 7.5 inches (19.05 cm).

The AMG V8 engine in the C43 has three valves per cylinder. Two valves take in the fuel, which is combusted by a dual ignition system. The third valve is used for **exhaust**.

Mercedes also uses the C43 AMG V8 engine in its off-road, sports-utility vehicle, the ML430.

## Intense headlights

*Xenon headlights are optional on the C43 AMG. Xenon is a gas-charged filament that produces a much stronger beam than ordinary headlights. Mercedes took great care when installing the xenon headlights so that they do not blind oncoming drivers.*

| | |
|---|---|
| **Chassis** | The supporting frame of the car on which the body is fixed. |
| **Exhaust** | Gas produced by burning fuel in the engine. |
| **Shock absorbers** | Devices that smooth out a bumpy ride. |

# Mercedes E55 AMG

**C**ritics have called the E55 AMG the "fastest and most exclusive sports sedan on the market." Like the C43, the E55 is an engineering and design collaboration between Mercedes and AMG. The car has been around since 1997 and it still has a strong reputation. Fast, high-tech, and luxurious, the E55 is an elite car. It has a top speed of 155 mph (249.4 km/h). Like the Cadillac STS and the Jaguar XJR, the E55 is no ordinary sedan.

## Vital Statistics for the 1998 E55 AMG

| | |
|---|---|
| Top speed: | 155 mph (249.4 km/h) |
| 0–60 mph: | 5.4 seconds |
| Engine: | V8 |
| Engine size: | 209.9 ci (3,439 cc) |
| Power: | 354 bhp at 5,500 rpm |
| Weight: | 3,600 lb. (1,633 kg) |
| Fuel economy: | 15 mpg |

Mercedes excelled in luxury and gadgetry with the E55. Leather seats and state-of-the-art electronic devices help make the inside of the car one of the most stylish ever designed.

## Milestones

### 1995

Mercedes launches the E-Class as a new range below the S-Class.

### 1996

In collaboration with AMG, Mercedes introduces the E50, which has a Mercedes body and an AMG engine.

### 1998

The E55 AMG becomes the latest in Mercedes' E-Class range. It has a powerful 24-valve V8 engine that AMG has designed to be highly fuel efficient and economical.

Well-weighted steering combined with the lowered, stiffened suspension, results in amazingly agile **handling** for such a giant. The massive brakes are among the world's best.

The largest model among the E55 range is the station wagon. AMG adapted the V8 of the sedan for the station wagon so that even though the station wagon is much heavier than the sedan, it is only 0.2 seconds slower than the sedan when sprinting from 0 to 60 mph (97 km/h).

**Handling**    The way in which a car responds to the actions of the driver.

# Specifications

The electronic gadgetry on the E55 is state of the art. For example, ultrasonic sensors on the front and rear bumpers help guide the driver while parking. There is also an Electronic Stability Program (ESP) to keep each wheel from spinning too quickly.

### Air bags

For greater passenger safety, the E55 AMG has eight **air bags**. Two of the air bags are located near the front. When inflated they cover the side windows to prevent shattered glass from hurting the occupants.

### Big, efficient engine

The E55 AMG has the biggest and one of the most efficient V8 engines of any Mercedes. Each cylinder is fitted with two **spark plugs** that fire quickly one after the other. This gives almost continuous combustion.

The headlights on the E55 AMG are oval shaped and have polycarbonate (strong plastic) lenses. There is also a high-pressured washing mechanism that cleans them.

The front and rear wheels are exceptionally large for a sedan. Each wheel is 18 inches (45.72 cm) in diameter. Inside the wheels are specially fitted vented disc brakes.

### Improved suspension

Thicker anti-roll bars and stiffer coil springs and shock absorbers give the E55 AMG the safest suspension system of almost any Mercedes. The changes, however, have not made the car ride any less smoothly.

### Hidden front wipers

*When not in use, the front windshield wipers are well hidden under the back of the hood. The speed of the wipers is adjustable, depending how heavy it is raining.*

### Spacious rear seats

*The back seats are roomy enough for three passengers to sit comfortably. The headrests also give added protection and comfort.*

| | |
|---|---|
| **Air bags** | Devices that inflate rapidly in an accident to protect people in the car. |
| **Spark plugs** | Devices in the engine that produce an electric charge to ignite fuel. |

# Mercedes A-Class

A t 38 mpg, the A-Class is a Mercedes that takes **fuel economy** seriously. The small and tall A-Class is an unusual shape, but the car's design combines efficient performance with plenty of room inside for four occupants. Not long after it was introduced, it was discovered that the A-Class could flip over when turning corners at high speed. Mercedes recalled all the models and quickly solved the problem. Today it is one of the world's oustanding small cars.

## Milestones

### 1996

Advertising campaigns begin all over Europe for Mercedes' A-Class, even though the car has not yet been built.

### 1997

The A-Class is launched, but critics discover that it has major safety flaws. The worst problem is that the car sometimes flips over when making sharp turns. Production ceases and all cars are recalled.

### 1998

The A-Class is relaunched. All safety issues have been fixed.

**Vital Statistics for the 1999 A-Class**

| | |
|---|---|
| Top speed: | *112 mph (180.2 km/h)* |
| 0–60 mph: | *11.1 seconds* |
| Engine: | *In-line four* |
| Engine size: | *97.52 ci (1,598 cc)* |
| Power: | *102 bhp at 5,250 rpm* |
| Weight: | *2,401 lb. (1,089 kg)* |
| Fuel economy: | *38 mpg* |

*Because the engine and transmission are mounted under the car, the A-Class has an unusually large interior for a small car.*

The engines in the A-Class cars are sweet and willing and very economical, thanks to high-top gearing, and the manual gearshift is delightfully short and precise.

The most expensive A-Class is the Avantgarde. It gives greater power and sharper handling than the other A-Class models. Critics, however, said it cost too much money for such a small car.

**Fuel economy**    How many miles a car can travel on a gallon of gas.

# Specifications

The A-Class is the perfect city car, able to park in small spaces and easy to drive. It is also a good people carrier, having plenty of leg and headroom. To get such ample space inside the car, the engine and transmission were placed underneath the floor.

**Low-mounted engine**

The specially designed engine and transmission are mounted under the floor level of the car to give more room in the tall interior.

**Spacious interior**

The interior of the A-Class is very roomy for such a small car. Near 70 percent of the car's length is given over to seating and luggage space.

 The front wheels on the A-Class are fitted with very good disc brakes. The rear wheels, however, have drum brakes. This is a common combination in many cars.

 The A-Class is not only Mercedes' first small car, it is also the company's first **front-wheel drive** car.

**Mercedes appearance**

If you look at the A-Class from the front, with the distinctive **grille**, sloped hood, and three-pointed star badge, it is unmistakably Mercedes-Benz.

## Tall car

*For a small car, the A-Class is very tall. Its height is 62 inches (157.5 cm), and on the inside there is 38.5 inches (97.79 cm) of head-room in the front seat.*

## Retractable soft top

*The soft roof can be pulled back to give the occupants an experience similar to riding in a convertible.*

**Front-wheel drive**   A car in which the engine drives the front wheels.

**Grille**   A grating at the front of a car that lets air in to cool the engine.

29

# Glossary

**aerodynamic** (AIR o dy NAM ik): Designed to pass smoothly through the air.

**chassis** (CHASS ee): The supporting frame of the car on which the body is fixed.

**disc brakes** (DISK BRAYKS): A type of brake with a rotating disc inside the wheel mechanism. A clip pinches the discs to stop the wheels.

**front-wheel drive** (FRUNT we ul DRYV): A car in which the engine drives the front wheels.

**fuel economy** (FYU el eh KON uh mee): How many miles a car can travel on a gallon of gas.

**roadholding** (RODE HOLD ing): A car's ability to grip the road without sliding.

**sedan** (seh DAN): A car with two or four doors and seats for four or more people.

**spark plug** (SPARK PLUG): Device in the cylinder head that produces an electric charge igniting fuel in the cylinder. The ignited fuel pushes down the piston in the cylinder rotating the crankshaft.

**supercharger** (SOO pur CHAR jur): A device that increases the air in the engine to help it burn fuel more efficiently.

**suspension** (sus PEN shun): *Spring system that supports a car and makes it travel more smoothly.*

**torque** (TORK): *The force produced by an engine to rotate the driveshaft of the car.*

**traction** (TRAK shun): *The grip between a tire and the surface of the road.*

**transmission** (trans MISH un): *Speed-changing gears that transmit power from the engine to the axle.*

**wheelbase** (WE ul BASE): *The distance between the front and back axles.*

# Further Information

## websites

www.cyberparent.com/wheels/mercedes.htm
History of Mercedes-Benz

http://auto.howstuffworks.com/engine.htm
How Stuff Works: Car Engines

www.mbca.org
Mercedes-Benz Club of America

www.mbusa.com/brand/index.jsp
Mercedes-Benz USA

## books

● Adler, Dennis. **Mercedes-Benz: 110 Years of Excellence.** Motorbooks International, 1995.

● Bacon, Roy. **Mercedes-Benz in Pictures.** Motorbooks International, 2001.

● Nitske, W. Robert. **Mercedes-Benz Production Models 1946–1995.** Motorbooks International, 1996.

● Sutton, Richard. **Eyewitness: Car.** Dorling Kindersley Publishing, 2000.

# *Index*